PICTURE LIBRARY

ASTRONAUTS

PICTURE LIBRARY
ASTRONAUTS

N.S. Barrett

Franklin Watts

London   New York   Sydney   Toronto

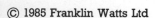

© 1985 Franklin Watts Ltd

First published in Great Britain
   1985 by
Franklin Watts Ltd
12a Golden Square
London W1

First published in the USA by
Franklin Watts Inc
387 Park Avenue South
New York
N.Y. 10016

First published in Australia by
Franklin Watts
1 Campbell Street
Artarmon, NSW 2064

UK ISBN: 0 86313 282 0
US ISBN: 0-531-10002-2
Library of Congress Catalog Card
Number: 85-50156

Printed in Italy

Designed by
Barratt & Willard

Photographs by
NASA
Novosti Press Agency

Illustration by
Mike Saunders

Technical Consultant
Robin Kerrod

Contents

Introduction   6

The space suit   8

Astronaut training   10

Living in space   13

Working in space   16

Meeting in space   22

Walking in space   23

Exploring other worlds   26

The story of astronauts   28

Facts and records   30

Glossary   31

Index   32

Introduction

Astronauts are the explorers of space. They are the men and women who travel in spacecraft, finding out what it is like to live and work in space.

Some astronauts have stayed in space for months at a time in spacecraft going around the Earth. Twelve astronauts have landed on the Moon and explored its surface.

△ The first man in space, Yuri Gagarin, strapped into position on the flight deck of Vostok 1. The first astronauts were pioneers, risking unknown dangers.

Most astronauts are either American or Soviet. The Soviets call their spacemen cosmonauts. On one mission the two nations met in space.

△ A modern astronaut, Bruce McCandless, at work outside the Space Shuttle.

The space suit

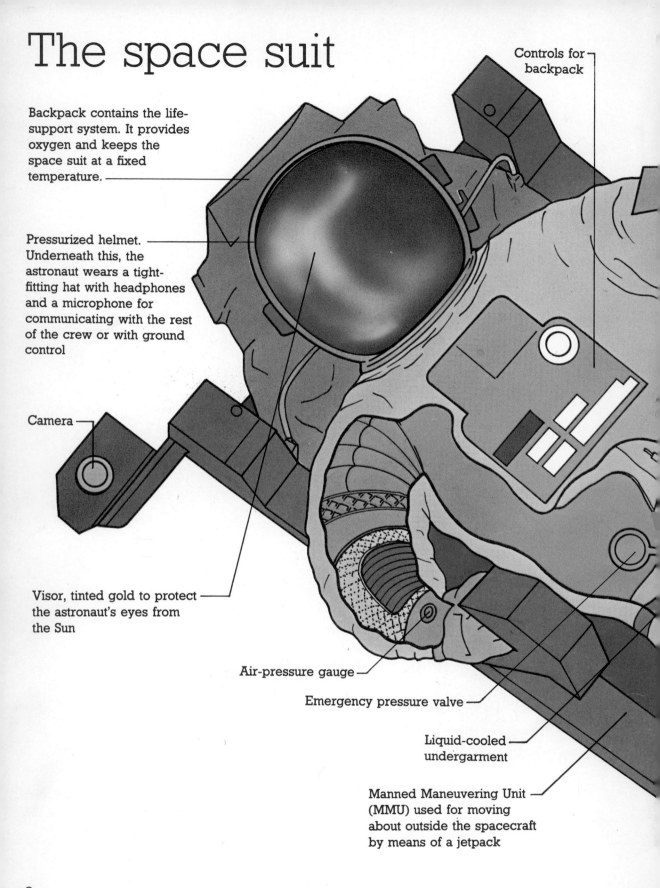

Backpack contains the life-support system. It provides oxygen and keeps the space suit at a fixed temperature.

Pressurized helmet. Underneath this, the astronaut wears a tight-fitting hat with headphones and a microphone for communicating with the rest of the crew or with ground control

Camera

Visor, tinted gold to protect the astronaut's eyes from the Sun

Controls for backpack

Air-pressure gauge

Emergency pressure valve

Liquid-cooled undergarment

Manned Maneuvering Unit (MMU) used for moving about outside the spacecraft by means of a jetpack

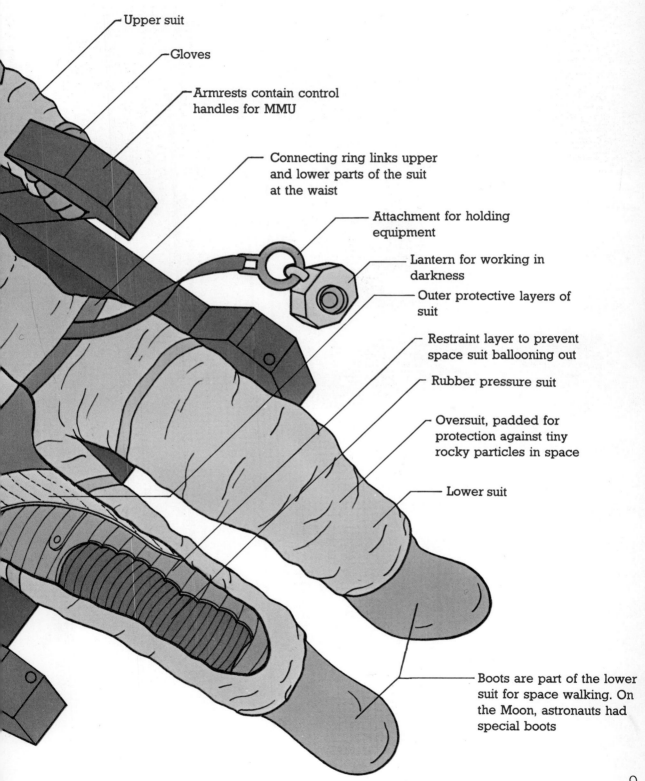

Upper suit

Gloves

Armrests contain control
handles for MMU

Connecting ring links upper
and lower parts of the suit
at the waist

Attachment for holding
equipment

Lantern for working in
darkness

Outer protective layers of
suit

Restraint layer to prevent
space suit ballooning out

Rubber pressure suit

Oversuit, padded for
protection against tiny
rocky particles in space

Lower suit

Boots are part of the lower
suit for space walking. On
the Moon, astronauts had
special boots

Astronaut training

The first astronauts were highly trained engineers and test pilots. Today's astronauts are also very skilled and in excellent physical condition. They usually have first-class qualifications in science, engineering or medicine.

Astronauts undergo special ground training to prepare them for living and working in space.

△ An astronaut gets accustomed to the flight deck controls in a Space Shuttle trainer.

▷ An astronaut is prepared for a session of underwater training to help him get used to the sensation of weightlessness.

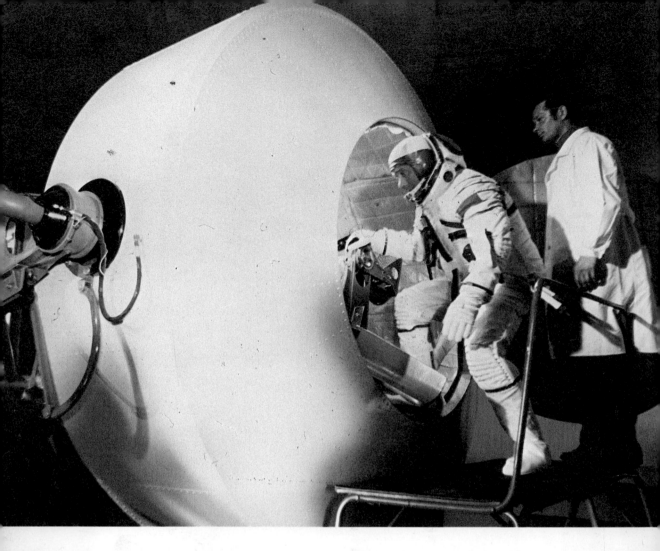

The skills needed to work outside a spacecraft are difficult to learn in training. Astronauts practice space walking underwater, but they develop the techniques in space.

Non-astronauts sometimes travel in the Space Shuttle, to work in the Spacelab for example. They do not need to go through such intensive training programs.

△ A cosmonaut enters a training centrifuge. This is a device that whirls the occupant around at great speed to accustom the person to the great force experienced at a rocket launch.

Living in space

In space, human beings are exposed to conditions that are very different from those on Earth. There is no air in space and no sensation of gravity and it is either much hotter or much colder than anywhere on Earth.

A spacecraft has its own supply of air and the temperature is regulated. But astronauts have to get used to the very strange feeling of weightlessness.

▽ Astronaut Charles Conrad enjoys a shower on a Skylab mission. Using liquid soap, he squirted warm water at himself from a water gun. This method created problems, because escaping water had to be vacuumed from the inside of the spacecraft. Astronauts on the Shuttle now have sponge baths.

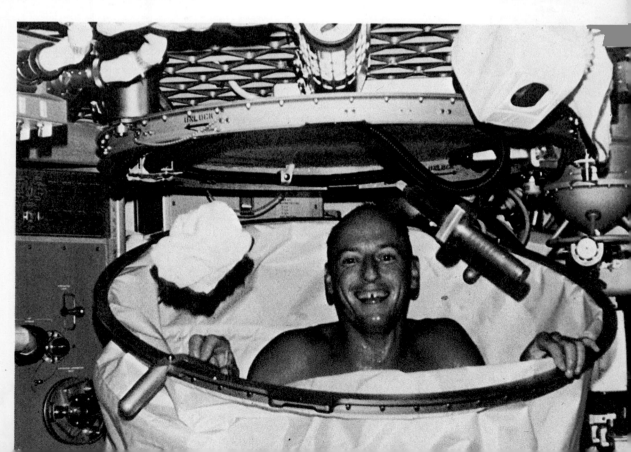

Spacecraft such as the Space Shuttle and the Soviet Salyut space stations enable astronauts to live and work in space in reasonable comfort.

Spacecraft systems protect the astronauts from the hazards of living in space. In 1984 cosmonauts spent nearly eight months in Salyut 7 with no ill effects.

△ Life aboard a Soviet space station. Three cosmonauts relax in Salyut 7.

◁ There is no floor or ceiling in space. Astronauts attach themselves to fixtures during a rest session so that they do not float around the cabin.

Working in space

Much of the work that astronauts do in space is experimental. They are still pioneers. They make new discoveries about space and help to pave the way for future missions.

Space programs cost billions of dollars, and each new step must be carefully planned. Each astronaut has specially allotted tasks to carry out.

▽ Astronaut Sally Ride talks to ground control from the flight deck of the Space Shuttle. An astronaut-scientist, Dr Ride became the first American woman in space when she flew on the seventh Shuttle mission, in 1983.

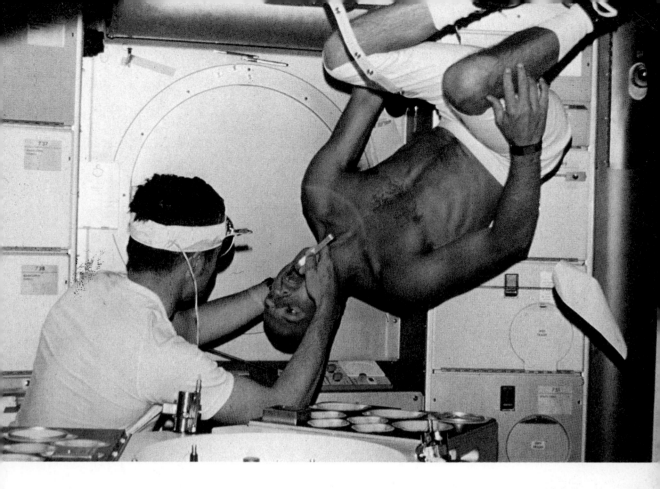

Spacecraft systems are controlled by computer. But astronauts must know how everything works and be prepared to take over in an emergency.

Many scientific experiments are carried out in space. The Space Shuttle often takes up scientists who are not fully trained astronauts. These may be payload specialists, who are experts in particular experiments.

△ Dr Joseph Kerwin gives fellow-astronaut Charles Conrad an oral examination. This might seem an unusual position, but it is a good example of how weightlessness in space can be an advantage.

Working outside a spacecraft is called extravehicular activity, better known as EVA or space walking. Astronauts on EVA wear special space suits. If they are not attached to the spacecraft, they use an MMU (Manned Maneuvering Unit).

Astronauts often work in the cargo bay of the Shuttle. Work outside the Shuttle includes repairs to spacecraft and the rescue of satellites that have gone wrong in space.

△ Astronaut Jack Lousma carrying out an experiment on a Skylab mission. Skylab was large enough for tests like this one, on a maneuvering unit, to be done without the risk of going outside. The MMU (Manned Maneuvering Unit) used today was developed from these experiments.

▷ Astronaut Dale Gardner uses an MMU to leave the Shuttle and capture a "lost" satellite.

▷ Bruce McCandless floats up out of the Shuttle cargo bay. McCandless was the first astronaut to float freely in space, untethered to a spacecraft.

The tests and exercises McCandless performed on this Shuttle mission were a dress rehearsal for the later flight in which two crippled satellites were rescued from space and brought back to Earth.

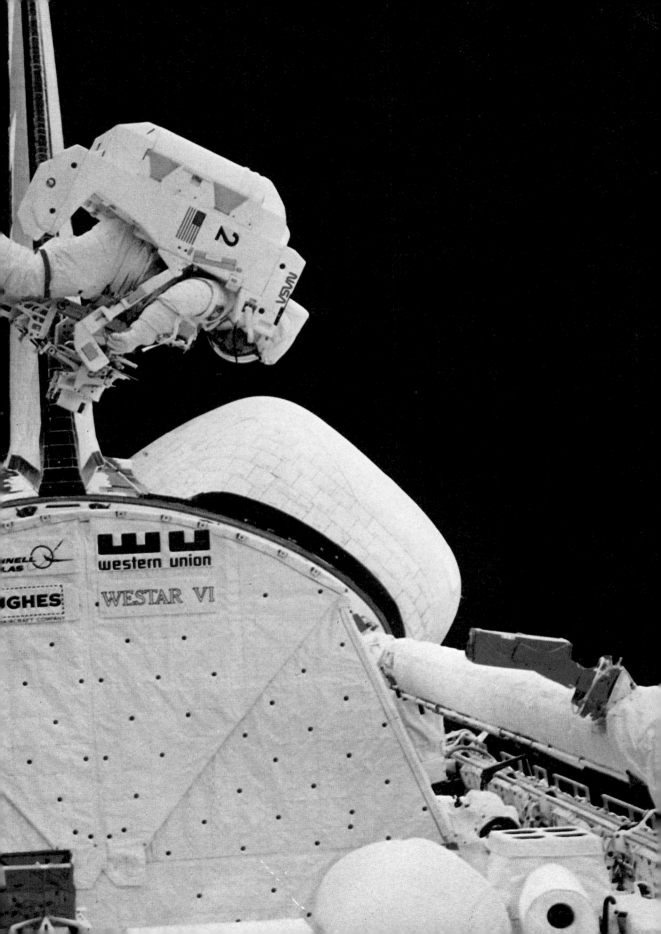

Meeting in space

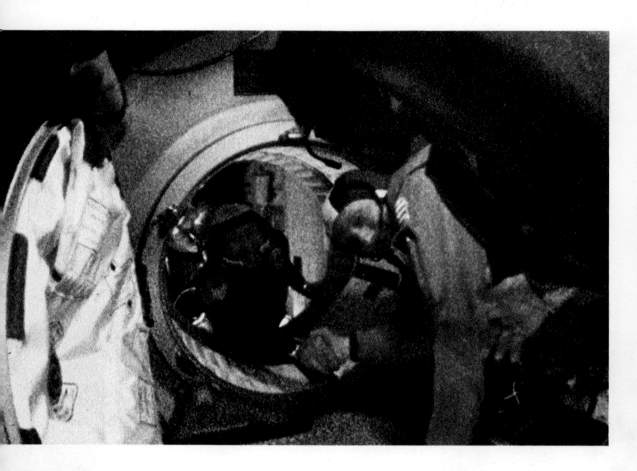

Docking is a maneuver in which two spacecraft join up in space. It is used, for example, when a spacecraft takes a change of crew to a space station.

The most famous meeting in space was in 1975. A Soviet Soyuz and an American Apollo spacecraft docked and stayed linked for one day.

△ A historic link-up in space. Apollo astronauts met Soyuz cosmonauts after the two spacecraft had docked. The picture shows Thomas Stafford shaking hands with Alexei Leonov through the interconnecting hatch. The spacemen visited each other's craft.

Walking in space

Space walking is a very specialized astronaut skill. Maneuvering in space is not as easy as it looks.

On the Shuttle, astronauts enter an airlock from the cabin to put on their space suits. Outside, they either work tethered to the Shuttle or use their jetpacks to move freely in space.

▽ There was plenty of extravehicular activity, or space walking, on the first Skylab mission. The astronauts had to carry out repairs to a damaged solar panel and rescue the project from disaster.

◁ Astronaut Ed White on the first American space walk. This took place in June 1965, just 11 weeks after Soviet cosmonaut Leonov had become the first man to float in space.

White stayed outside for about 20 minutes, twice as long as Leonov, and used a hand-held thruster, or gas gun, to maneuver. He enjoyed the experience so much that he was reluctant to return to the Gemini spacecraft.

Exploring other worlds

Landing astronauts on the Moon was a truly amazing and exciting achievement. Yet it was only a tiny journey in space. So far, we have been able to explore other planets only with unmanned spacecraft.

A manned mission to Mars might be possible before the end of the century. Travel to the stars would need much more powerful rockets than are available at present.

▽ The tracks of the astronauts' hand cart can be seen leading away from the landing craft of the Apollo 14 mission. The cart helped the astronauts to travel farther than on the first two missions. On later missions they used a rover or Moon buggy.

Six Apollo missions each landed two astronauts on the Moon. They set down on different parts of the Moon to explore its surface.

The first Moon astronauts were limited to exploring small areas, because they had to walk. Astronauts on the last three missions carried more supplies of air, food and water and used special vehicles. They were therefore able to travel much farther afield.

△ Astronaut Buzz Aldrin sets up an experiment on the first Apollo mission. The instruments left on the Moon continued to send information back to Earth for years afterwards.

The story of astronauts

First man in space

The story of astronauts began on the morning of April 12, 1961, when a Soviet spacecraft, Vostok 1, was launched into orbit around the Earth. Aboard the spacecraft was Major Yuri Gagarin, who thus became the first man in space.

Gagarin made one orbit and touched down less than two hours after the liftoff. Previous Soviet launches had put dogs into space and brought them back again.

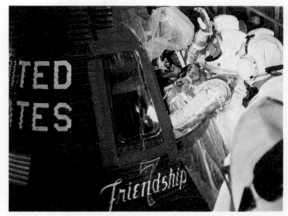
△ John Glenn and his space capsule *Friendship 7*.

became the first American in space, with a 15-minute suborbital flight. Then, in February 1962, John Glenn became the first American astronaut to orbit the Earth. He made three orbits in the Mercury capsule *Friendship 7*.

△ Soviet heroes Yuri Gagarin and Valentina Tereshkova.

The pioneers

All astronauts are pioneers of manned spaceflight. This was particularly true of the first astronauts, who faced many unknown dangers in space.

A few weeks after Gagarin's historic flight, Alan Shepard

△ Before the Space Shuttle program, returning American spacecraft parachuted down to the ocean, where they were recovered.

Cosmonaut milestones

The Soviets notched up more notable space "firsts" when they launched the first woman in space and the first spacecraft to carry more than one cosmonaut. Valentina Tereshkova made her flight in Vostok 6, in June 1963. In October 1964, Voskhod 1 took up not two, but three, cosmonauts.

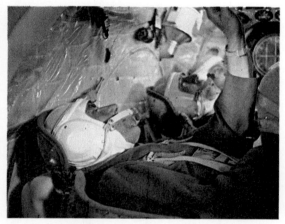

△ The three-man crew of Voskhod 1 lies strapped to their couches. Voskhod 1 was the first spacecraft to carry more than one man.

Moon mission

Three weeks after Alan Shepard led American astronauts into space, President John F. Kennedy announced a plan to put a man on the Moon before the end of the 1960s. The Apollo Project, a daring and dramatic space program,

succeeded on July 20, 1969, when astronaut Neil Armstrong climbed down from the Apollo 11 lunar module *Eagle* and set foot on the Moon.

Further steps in space

In the early 1970s, the Soviets launched the first of their Salyut space stations and the American Skylab missions were carried out. The Salyut crews stayed aloft for long periods and were often visited for short spells by cosmonauts taken up in Soyuz spacecraft.

In 1975, Apollo and Soyuz spacecraft linked up in space.

△ The Three Apollo 11 astronauts return to a period of quarantine.

But this was the last US manned mission until the start of the Shuttle program in 1981. The Shuttle has made it possible for many more people to become space travelers.

Facts and records

Accidents in space

Considering the dangers involved, there have not been many accidents in space. But a few tragic mishaps have caused the deaths of spacemen.

The first of these occurred during a launch pad test of an Apollo spacecraft in January 1967. An electrical problem started a fire in the oxygen-filled command module, and three astronauts were burned to death. They were Ed White, who had made the first American space walk, Virgil Grissom, who had nearly drowned on a previous mission,

△ Astronaut John Young at the controls of the Space Shuttle.

and Roger Chaffee.

Three months later, Vladimir Komarov died in a crash landing when the parachute lines of Soyuz 1 became entangled. Three more cosmonauts were killed in 1971, when the pressure in Soyuz 11 failed on its return to Earth.

Veteran spaceman

When astronaut John Young went up on the first Space Shuttle flight, in 1981, it was his fifth time in space – a record.

Longest time in space

A space endurance record was set by three cosmonauts in 1984. Leonid Kizim, Vladimir Solovyov and Oleg Atkov spent 237 days aboard the Salyut 7 space station.

△ The memorial plaque left on the Moon after the first landing.

Glossary

Backpack
The complete life-support system carried on an astronaut's back, when outside the spacecraft.

Cosmonaut
What the Soviets call an astronaut.

Docking
Joining up with another spacecraft.

EVA
Extravehicular activity, or work outside a spacecraft.

Gravity
The pull exerted by one body on another. Spacecraft are kept in orbit by the pull of the Earth's gravity.

Liftoff
The moment when a spacecraft leaves the launch pad.

MMU
Manned Maneuvering Unit. This is the device an astronaut uses to move around outside the spacecraft.

Orbit
The path one body takes around another. A spacecraft might travel in an orbit around the Earth or the Moon. The Earth orbits the Sun.

Solar panel
An array of cells that uses the Sun's rays to produce electricity for powering a spacecraft.

Space Shuttle
One of the fleet of American spacecraft that separates from its rockets and fuel tank and returns to Earth like a plane after each mission.

Space station
A spacecraft that stays in orbit for a long period and is visited by other spacecraft which often bring a change of crew.

Spacelab
A special scientific laboratory that is carried on some Space Shuttle missions.

Space walking
Same as EVA.

Weightlessness
The sensation of not being pulled toward Earth that astronauts feel in space. They feel as if they have no weight.

Index

Aldrin, Buzz 27
Apollo 22, 26, 27, 29, 30
Armstrong, Neil 2, 29

backpack 8, 31
boots 9

cargo bay 20
centrifuge 12
Chaffee, Roger 30
Conrad, Charles 13, 17
cosmonaut 7, 12, 15, 22, 28, 29, 31

docking 22, 31

Earth 6, 13
EVA 18, 31

Gagarin, Yuri 6, 28
Gardner, Dale 19
Gemini 25
Glenn, John 28
gravity 13, 31
Grissom, Virgil 30

helmet 8

jetpack 9, 23

Kennedy, John F. 29
Kerwin, Joseph 17
Komarov, Vladimir 30

Leonov, Alexei 22, 25
liftoff 31
Lousma, Jack 18

McCandless, Bruce 7, 20, 21
MMU 9, 18, 19, 31
Moon 6, 26, 27, 29, 30

orbit 31

payload specialist 17
pressure suit 8

Ride, Sally 16

Salyut 15, 29, 30
Shepard, Alan 28, 29
shower 13
Skylab 13, 18, 29
solar panel 23, 31
Soyuz 22, 29, 30
Spacelab 12, 31
Space Shuttle 7, 10, 12, 14, 15, 16,
     20, 21, 23, 29, 30, 31
space station 22, 31
space suit 8, 9, 18, 23
space walking 12, 18, 23, 25, 31
Stafford, Thomas 22

Tereshkova, Valentina 28, 29
training 10, 11

visor 8
Voskhod 29
Vostok 6, 28, 29

weightlessness 10, 13, 17, 31
White, Ed 24, 25, 30

Young, John 30